Praise for *Unburying the Bones*

In her debut poetry collection, *Unburying the Bones*, Victoria Buitron dresses untamed desire with the body of a broken marriage, gives it hair, sex, and crowns it with childlessness, all this as a quiet, lyrical rage traces the history of the everyday violence bruising the lives of countless women. She asks: "How can I heal if my mother only taught me to reside in the place between praying and wishing?" And it is precisely this "place between praying and wishing" that Buitron sets on fire, this place of false security, false comfort, false patriarchal narrative. By the light of this fire, these poems call us to birth a "new skin" and to love ourselves again "when no one sees." Read these poems and bear witness to the courageous act of reclaiming one's life.

—**Octavio Quintanilla**, VERSOFRONTERA SERIES EDITOR AND AUTHOR OF *THE BOOK OF WOUNDED SPARROWS* AND *LAS HORAS IMPOSIBLES / THE IMPOSSIBLE HOURS*

When a mother bear asked, *How do you do it?... Live with Men*, Victoria Buitron's bearing reply is a manifesto of poesy that unveils her quest to recapture the unquiet of womanhood, every man must read. *Unburying the Bones* is an excavation of matriarchy digging to rediscover the sacrosanct of self. The collection disentangles the complexities of patriarchy, sexuality, marriage and esteem to unfurl (while inhaling the dulcet of palo santo) that *healing is like roots from a tree seeking out water.* Who amongst us doesn't need water?

—**Frederick-Douglass Knowles II**, HARTFORD POET LAUREATE EMERITUS AND AUTHOR OF *SINKING IN MOONLIGHT ALONE*

Victoria Buitron aims to teach us what we already know, deep down: there are one thousand ways to come home, but we spend most of our lives on a pilgrimage back to ourselves at our most alive and various. Her debut poetry collection *Unburying the Bones* reads as a field guide to the natural world—inclusive of the body and of the creature world that consoles it. Let it be the antidote to all that would bury us.

—**Carol Ann Davis**, AUTHOR OF *SONGBIRD*

Unburying the Bones is unrelenting and astonishing. These poems overflow—erupt!—with passion and expression, a dynamism of form and sound and theme from howl to whisper, from betrayal, desire, and revenge to recognition and reclamation: of female pleasure and agency, of kinship with the more-than-human—from deer and jay to the Milky Way—and ultimately of a body whole: tender skin, suckling blood, and bones, too, which the poet reminds us can grow outside our bodies, too. These poems will change you.

—**Ana Maria Spagna**, AUTHOR OF *MILE MARKER SIX*

Unburying the Bones

Unburying the Bones

Poems

Victoria Buitron

VERSOFRONTERA, NO. 1
Selected by Octavio Quintanilla

TRP: THE UNIVERSITY PRESS OF SHSU
HUNTSVILLE, TEXAS 77341

Note from the author: The book is comprised of poems. They should not be considered fiction or nonfiction, but whatever exists in between.

Library of Congress Cataloging-in-Publication Data

Names: Buitron, Victoria, author.
Title: Unburying the bones : poems / Victoria Buitron.
Other titles: VersoFrontera (Series) ; no. 1.
Description: First edition. | Huntsville, Texas : TRP: The University Press of SHSU, [2025] | Series: VersoFrontera ; no. 1
Identifiers: LCCN 2025023466 (print) | LCCN 2025023467 (ebook) | ISBN 9781680034462 (trade paperback) | ISBN 9781680034479 (ebook)
Subjects: LCSH: Grief in women--Poetry. | Women--Crimes against--Poetry. | Misogyny--Poetry. | Matrilineal kinship--Poetry. | LCGFT: Poetry.
Classification: LCC PS3602.U3826 U53 2025 (print) | LCC PS3602.U3826 (ebook) | DDC 811/.6--dc23/eng/20250530
LC record available at https://lccn.loc.gov/2025023466
LC ebook record available at https://lccn.loc.gov/2025023467

FIRST EDITION

Cover art by Anna Bogush | Shutterstock
Author photo by Juliette Páez Tobar

Cover design by Cody Gates, Happenstance Type-O-Rama
Interior design by Maureen Forys, Happenstance Type-O-Rama

Printed and bound in the United States of America
First Edition Copyright: 2025

TRP: The University Press of SHSU
Huntsville, Texas 77341
texasreviewpress.org

For all my past selves

Contents

Part I

Part II

Tendré una hija rota
y la peinaré con todos mis dientes.

I will have a broken daughter
and brush her hair with all my teeth.

MÓNICA OJEDA

Part I

Grief Ceremony

In absence of saying
he touched me and thus
a cop, and thus a statement,
and thus retellings of saliva,

and thus the court,
and thus the questions
of how there were no screams
but why I sought my own silence

and thus no conviction,
thus I've known my voice is not evidence,
and thus I make my own grief ceremony where

I chew on mint leaves
and wear a lone cardinal
on the ripe skin of my ear

feast on smoke rings
to tire burns in under-tongue scent,
tap my toe meat on rust monarch dirt,

say a prayer,
if not a prayer then a plea
if not a plea then a miracle
does not mean they will always
check the trunk to see if my shout is there.

A Review of My Birth Control Methods

Depo-Provera

I get a shot by my navel every three months.
        One day, a nurse asks: "Do you remember me?"
I don't want to know anyone at Planned Parenthood.
        I want light banter, and *you're all set.*
        But this person—with a scar on her forehead
        and almond-shaped eyes—destroys the fantasy.
Then I remember as she swabs the alcohol near my navel;
I swapped blood with her once.
We made a cut on our palms, shook them,
and promised we'd always be friends.
        That was before I moved thousands of miles away,
        before years passed, before I came back.
        We catch up as she slides in the injection.
        She's married, with kids. I'm married—without.
        A summary of leavings and goings in a few minutes.
I apologize for not recognizing her, my once blood sister.
I have a new phone number when I leave,
        and wonder who will reach out first,
        but I'm sure that the answer will be no one.

Pills

I know the theory   but can't complete the execution.
Too many *oops, I forgot again.*   Days will pass without taking them,
and then I'll proceed to gulp them up   like prescription painkillers.

Condoms

Y J N M I A U G B C W D B N P U I L T J J D O
R F D I G U V E U S X T W E Q O Y W D N T L H
T V I C I G R E L L A Z T H M J T Y E N U P I
N L F L M S Z I S U R G I C A L E M C G M D E
E T R U M T K X T W H J H J X L W U R M L Z W
T S X H W E M T H M F N Y E R U S A E L P G O
F A I A L A F X I N Y K C U N K A V A M J E D
O Q F C T L D J N Z X X Q O Q O V P S S L Q Q
T S U O V T W G N Y M G U M F Z T D E X E V J
U E O H E H Q U E T N A C I R B U L D Q B H R
O B Z R T I D Q S Y A C L K R I S K R D K E E
E M E T A N F W S I C T I H K F U W E Y U V Q
E V T Y H G K D I N Q O H A Y C K L F B B O N
R M O D E C U D E R N O I T A S N E S V Q L K
H U T B T M U E L O R T E P R K E P L Z J G C
T H W W N G C B W Z L M K Q O L H M J W H X W

Find the following words. If you find any additional words, you're just seeing what you want to see. Words are hidden as follows: ↑↓→←↘

ALLERGIC	THINNESS	SURGICAL	PLEASURE
PETROLEUM	DECREASED	GLOVE	RISK
LUBRICANT	SENSATION	REDUCED	STEALTHING

IUD

I've never been pregnant or given birth,
but I decide to try it anyway.
Nurse Who Is Not My Blood Sister
says being on my period for the insertion helps.
It'll hurt less, but it feels like it's swelling
as it's pushed in, then the implant becomes a fishhook,
my uterus trying to make space for the stab.
Nope, she says. *Too tight*.
Her gloves are splattered in blood. I think of sliced cherries.
She tries one more time, and even though this is the opposite of giving birth,
I make a note to ask a friend if the two feelings are related.
My blood drips on the examination table.
My vagina fails to relax and receive.

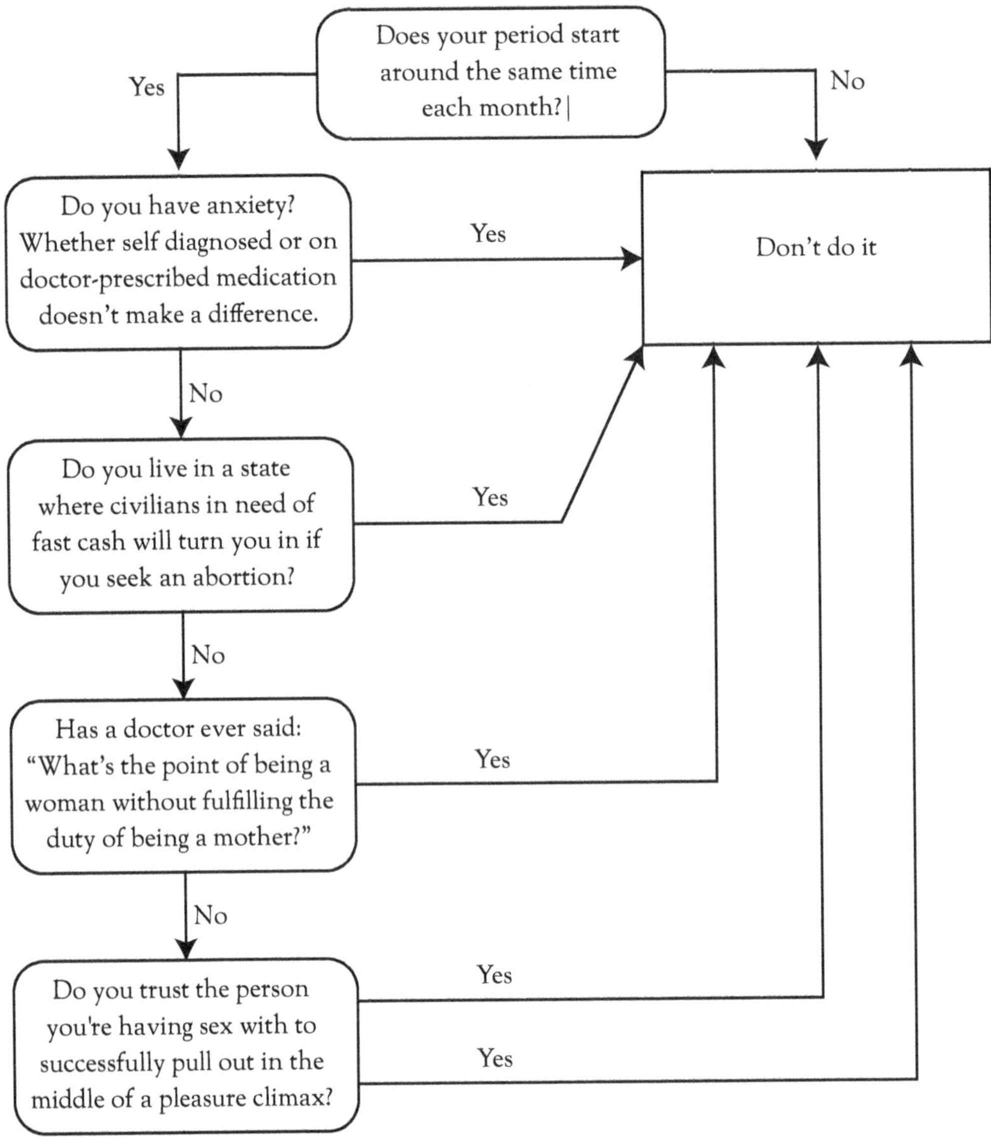
Does your period start around the same time each month?
Yes
No
Do you have anxiety? Whether self diagnosed or on doctor-prescribed medication doesn't make a difference.
Yes
Don't do it
No
Do you live in a state where civilians in need of fast cash will turn you in if you seek an abortion?
Yes
No
Has a doctor ever said: "What's the point of being a woman without fulfilling the duty of being a mother?"
Yes
No
Do you trust the person you're having sex with to successfully pull out in the middle of a pleasure climax?
Yes
Yes

Nexplanon

I didn't know there would be anesthesia.
I didn't know there would be blood.
I didn't know my arm would bruise Rorschach.
I didn't know the army greens and deep blues would last so long.
I didn't know my husband would refuse to place a finger
on the tiny bar that can be felt by touching my skin.
I didn't know how much this would upset me.
I didn't know I'd want to say: *I sacrificed my time,*
and my health, and my arm, and all the symptoms that come with it,
and you won't even touch it.
I wanted him to know how it felt.
He did it, eventually, shivered when he touched,
as if the bump on my skin punctured his muscle and not mine.

Outercourse

I think something is wrong with me
because I can come with fingers, tongues,
and rubbing but not with a shaft inside me.
When I learn research studies have found
that anywhere from 30% to 80% of women
report that they cannot reach climax through penetrative sex, I feel less alone.
My husband learns that I don't need him inside me.
That we can do without hormones and latex
and punctures on my skin to avoid having children *and* still feel pleasure.
He licks my areolas, works counterclockwise on my clit, pulls me toward him.
And the best part is I don't worry about percentages
or if the condom is still on or about my period or lack of it
or the thick lining of my uterus.
I don't worry and I come.

An Etymology

I feed jasmine to the alligator doe,
and we swap nightmare stories
to release the oxymoron—
I ask if she knows the definition
of herself, and she says she doesn't need to.

On the walk back to my cabin,
the hyena doe shows me her mock penis,
and I reach in to stop her breach birth,
feel around for a snout and
blood purples my wrists
until the shrieks solve into whimpers.
She does not say thank you
but licks my knuckles clean.

Beyond the meadow is a panther doe,
belly sunned, tail twirls in the shape of candor,
and before I pass she defangs
her pinky paw with incisors, gives it to me,
the nerve ending still warm.

How do you know it'll grow back? I ask.
She says silly doe human,
and I thank her and leave.
Sharp enough that before I'm home,
I've slit my lobule—and there is no ache
because as a baby I learned to become
a girl who would become a woman
who refuses to feel pain.

A honey badger doe waits on my porch
next to the firewood, and she asks me
how many men I killed today.
And I say just one,
but I helped bring a hyena earth side,
so I'd say it's even.

Daddy's Lesson

I don't remember the blood.
Nor if the rock felt sanded
by an ancient ocean or if
loose pebbles were left on
my palm. All I remember
is his mom saying that
he had it coming.

If the cut didn't scare
him much, the stitches
would teach him, alright.
My dad loves to tell the story.
He always starts with the catalyst:
my Disney lunchboxes.

I break two in a month.
When he asks why, I confess
it's not me. A boy uses his fists
& kicks until the food leaks
through the cracks. Dad says
if Pablito tries that shit again,
grab a rock, swing toward his face.

He'll hit me himself if Ariel &
Jasmine come back home broken again.
Today he says that he didn't really think I'd do it.
That of course he'd never hit me,
but he couldn't let his only daughter
grow up to be afraid of boys. Of him?
Yes. But other boys? Never.

An Introduction to Poetry

tell the woodpecker to peck
your spine until constellations

confuse a whistle with a thrush's
sermon through a dawn mourning

see a kit lose its mother, heed peeps
of bewail, while fireworks plunder

rescue a fledgling from a blue jay
or decide to witness an instinct

converse with a raven, perhaps argue,
about its once incessant enemies

drown your questions beachside
as a seagull height drops oysters

paint with earthcolors and seaweed
by the perennial osprey nest

bear the hasty weight of the baby
barred owl's hollow matte eyes

eavesdrop on the wild parakeets'
gossip while you drink the low tide

decipher the word *wildness* while
a chosen bird tattoos your breast

Corpse Dress

I'm driving my dress to cocoon it under swaths of black licorice. Or to drown it beneath branches of fig trees while I suck on sugar cane, waiting until my gums bleed from the sweetness. Someone suggested I donate it. Sell it. My intuition was to stick it in a barrel, flood it with Cabernet Sauvignon from Maipú and leave the wood to shatter at the end of a waterfall. Shoot it with pellets that will plant tulips in the tight threads, and place it in my garden until critters make it into a mud castle the size of my clavicle. Axe throws that will cleave its pear shape until all that's left are shreds. Maybe smear it in pulp-free blood orange juice and coconut piña coladas. I decide to strap it to the back of my car, catching glimpses as it waves with the wind as a white flag. When I get to the trailhead, I put it on, clasp the front of it into a knot so I don't trip and leave the back to raze the ground like Hector's once gorgeous face—a collector of twigs and pebbles—my body as strong as Achille's, my will as weak as his heel. Even though there's no sun, just a drab sky, my sweat leaves the dress wet. When I get to the summit, I think about throwing it off the edge. Walking down in underwear and skin, leaving the woods to gulp it, for an osprey to make it part of its nest. But I head with the dress still on, not nearly as soiled as I thought it'd be. I find a camping spot. Start a fire. I take out the marshmallows, hover them over the blaze until the sugar honeys brown. Then stick them to the dress until the garment is sweetmeat, and I rope it up high to a tree. A bear comes, scoffs at my boots, sniffs my elbows, and climbs the tree to steal my past and almost future. I envision her licking the goo from her claws, taking the candied gunk and leaving the threads. Keeping it as a relic in her shelter, and I wish—as I'm left with a flicker of flames—what's next could come in a blink of hibernation, that my heart could stall for months like hers, eyes closed and body numb, to wake when snapdragons outlive the crude snow.

Inherited Rituals

A collaborative piece with Grecia Huesca Dominguez

We don't sip ayahuasca here, instead the witch gives my mother a glass bottle with distinct herbs to bury in our garden. While ants crawl and the worms wiggle among the dirt, my mom's desires made physical are also present. I love the vagueness of her pedidos, how they encompass everything: Stop my daughter from being sad, let me remain close to my husband although he's thousands of miles away, let my son be happy while getting over the death of his dog.

*

Sometimes I try to talk to my mother about my feelings and I hurt hers instead. When I asked about the times she took me to the curandera, she says it was because I never ate. For as long as I can remember, my body has never been enough. Always too something. Too skinny, too fat, too much like my mother's, too sick, too far from the place where I was born. For so long, my mother tried to fix my body.

*

Mami will never see the buried bottle again; her prayers are gathered by the earth, coalescing until they come alive. Nearby, sprouting from the ground next to her desires, is a sábila plant—aloe. It'll strip away the harmful energy of whoever walks beyond the threshold of our house. My mother has to keep it alive as if it were one of her children.

*

When I was little, she'd feed me all kinds of home remedies, supplements, vitamins, and natural juices. She'd take me to the curandera and the old lady would burn a hard, stale tortilla and pray over me with the smoke swirling all around me so I'd eat more. When I still didn't eat enough, my mother would sit next to radio in the morning and listen to a homeopath talk about the benefits of different herbs, teas, and infusions that might finally give me hunger. She'd go to the store and buy de-wormer to cleanse me from inside out. She'd feed me a tablespoon of olive oil and salt, she'd try to feed me an oatmeal smoothie, she'd try and try to feed me.

*

We visited a river with a shaman to beg the earth some more. I sat in a freezing puddle, the water the flowing vestiges of once snow, reaching just below my belly button. There was no cleanse with sugar, pulp oranges, or soda that my mother was usually asked to do. We let the cold placate us, and the shaman asked us to leave a gift to the river. My mother and I left our rings, but I wish I had left a lock of hair. A piece of my body left for another body, sitting next to the one that I came from and pieced together my bones.

*

The first time I felt fat, I was 11 years old. I don't remember the first time I went on a diet, but I was 16 when I asked my mother to take me to Jenny Craig. I prayed for my body to change. I wonder if this is how my mother prayed when she'd take me to the curandera. Hoping this time, we'd have found the solution to my problems. That maybe this ritual or concoction or diet would be the one to fix my latest bodily affliction. When I was 20 years old, I lost 30 pounds in three months because I couldn't eat. Cramps caused by IBS would keep me up at night crying because the pain was so intense. For a whole summer I ate half a turkey, tomato, and cheddar sandwich for breakfast and the other half for lunch. At night in between sobs, I prayed for my pain to go away, and yet every day I'd get more compliments about my changing body.

*

How can I heal if my mother only taught me to reside in the place between praying and wishing? These days I am trying to heal rather than fix myself. A fix is done once—all done, see, all fixed—and healing is slow like roots from a tree seeking out water, heat, space to grow deep in the earth. To grow wide as my body desires because that's how it prays now. It knows that fixing it is as useless as telling a river it needs to curve.

Nature's Classroom

They made us slice a sheep's eye before pretending we were enslaved. I wanted to lick the tapetum—a sheet of turquoise luminescence in the eyeball's lined back. A foil silver finish to see better in the dark. Humans lack it, our eyes more akin to a pig's. My crush cut between the cornea and optic nerve with a scalpel. No powdered gloves, vinyl stuck to skin. We never asked our middle names, only dissected tissue of what once breathed, learned our anatomy with parts of a dead animal seeped in formaldehyde. Sclera, extrinsic muscle, fatty tissue, vitreous humor. The moon's light was missing that night. He wore a plum shirt, forgot a jacket on his bunk bed. Peppermint skin, crinkled October leaves under our sneakers, almost-teen bodies in long double lines. We walked, shoulder to funny bone. Guided by costume-clad men and candlelight on a window. A pretend sheriff stroked a whip. Maybe I conjured the whip. Maybe it was a toy rifle. Maybe it was a sclera-white hand. A voice enjoyed our bowed heads, his face recalled as an abrasion with a Hulihee beard. We hid in a cabin, hunched shoulders and whispers, and used dim laughter to cloak quasi fear born from role play. A simulation to feel what those in the Underground Railroad felt. But how could a few hours and white men shouting reflect pain seeped in hundreds of years. This thought came years later, not as quick as the brain swaps bended light on our retinas. I was eleven. That night sheep and pig eyes jiggled in my cerebrum, the ooze that pooled on the dissecting pan from earlier in the day a gelatinous black hole behind the Milky Way. I wanted to leave by walking on stars and have dirt fall on my hair like sprinkle dust, let our eyes shine pearl when aimed by flashlight, to trace the lines of my crush's palms with no need to be freed from camp counselors by day, bounty hunters by night.

Not Saturn Devouring His Son

Mami fed the close-eyed babes
herself, far away from where they
first searched for a teat, & in the
leading to and after the birth,
my mother wouldn't let me
near Minnie, afraid she'd leave
a trail of stitches on my cheek,
& I was too young to explain to
Mami my dog would never hurt me.

Years later, on a day of sudden
confession, Mami said Minnie would
eat her newborns—Ops devouring
her old and new flesh—no snout
grasps on tender skin, a lone desire
to become sole again, to swallow
instinct & bones, to pink milk with
her very own suckling blood.

Even Beyoncé Said She Raised Her Man*

from another woman whose nipples he sucked,
but not the same way he was spoon-fed relish;
teach him to toil thighs with violet supper.
Malaise is no body, and rest? For locusts.
Stop. Listen. hey—li sten, let go of the blade—
if you let go, you can braise my pink toes.
The school calls & he's used spit as a weapon.
This milk weighs the same as the stakes he stole,
blaze his camo pillow & street pajamas,
hide the skullcap sword so there's no hurt.
A man is no child unless you desire
mazes of mother & red-eye midnight gazes.
At an empty nest all there's left: shell morsels.
He raises me to become a house of slaughter.

*After her version of *Jolene*

Tell me

a lamentation that
will not douse me in
kerosene, or a way to
mold my cradle of
abandonment into a
susurrus outside of my aorta,
how to tug teeth without
having a stranger touch
them, show me the difference
between telling and sowing,
if I knew already I could tell
apart a Black Racer from
a Copperhead, tell me, tell me,
before I caress the wrong snake.

Fragile

He says I'm too fragile,
not my body but my mind,
I wish I could break the way
he wants me to,
maybe in the crush of a car pileup
or a tumble down the stairs.
Instead, vultures feast on my brain
through the eyes, eating the meat,
leaving my skull and bones intact.
He comes home,
finds me in a fetal position
on my side of the bed,
my vultures invisible to him,
and asks when I last showered

How to Sleep Alone as a Woman

Check every room before bed *something heavy against the door* top floor only *car keys* dogs *creaky doors* baseball bat *car alarm* boat air horn *muscle relaxers* overinflated ego *phone ready* long metal flashlight *me encomiendo a Dios* no ground floor *extra locks on door* I pretend the world is a nice place *charged phone* leave a light on *check the closets* check the windows *check the door locks* a hammer under my bed *knowing I'll win a fight* never the first floor *door wedges* scissors *big dogs* melatonin *loaded gun near my bed* alarms *ambien* lying on my bed *getting ready* ready? *get ready* ready to ~~rest~~

Natasha Romanoff Died Because She Had No Kids or Spouse (Featuring Erasure)

In a helicopter, Natasha and her sister	her
joke about their forced hysterectomies	hysterectomies
and that's how I know I'm watching a movie,	know
not from the explosions	the
or poor Russian accents	accents
or metaphors for the Cold War,	for
but women laughing hundreds of feet in the air	
about the choice of becoming	choice
mothers taken from them.	.
Natasha says she has two families,	say lies
neither tied to her by blood, but by want.	tied blood want.
When the Black Widows	the
and her pseudo family leave her,	
a sea of women with barren uteruses rise,	barren
plucked by men who wanted them to serve as	plucked men as
weapons, puppets. Always dressed in black,	weapons, Always in
grieving their wombs.	grieving wombs.
If *widow* is used for a woman who lost a spouse,	for a spouse,
what's the noun to describe losing a body part	losing a body part
that's invisible to others?	to others?
When I leave the theater, the difference	I leave
between *childless* and *childfree* wades into my thoughts,	*childless* and *childfree*
but then I remember even women	I remember
with no children are taught	no
to sacrifice their lives for everyone else.	to sacrifice heir for everyone else.

"Greenwich municipal worker who photographed body of homicide victim Valerie Reyes demoted by town"

Mainstream Outlets

Let's drive by the
murderer's house,
his steely mustang's
ribs stick out, a rampike
through skin.

No trespassing signs
on skull-soaked grass,
nine bodies in search of
a teal-eyed one,
a woman missed first,
then missing.

Never deemed missing if
they are past runaways
with a record of mugshots
or with tired half-moon neck
tattoos etched on skin
darker than honey.

It takes cherry-blonde hair
and an online travel-lover
presence, photogenic selfies
with sham smiles to become
the only missing woman
in the United States.
Her body is home now,
but not all of last year's 268,884
missing women and girls
whose pictures were
never shown on the six,
eight,
eleven o'clock news.

Game Over

Wearing white is like carving a bullseye on our bodies, inviting men to spray us just so they can peek at our nipples or the floral etches of our bras, which means the first rule is never to wear white, light pink, or the soft yellow of newborn chicks. While it's better to steal one of our brother's vintage-whatever-concert t-shirts, we don't want to be confused for tomboys. We still wear our own shorts and tank tops, as long as we don't mind that these clothes might become trash after the hoopla, since there's a chance they'll be stained by ink or foam or mud water, or, although we hope not—drain water and piss. Another rule is that we ignore babies, toddlers, people in wheelchairs, and the elderly. Everyone else is game. The third is under no circumstances do we leave our homes in sandals. Sandals provide no traction even when dry, and once soaked—forget it—the soles of our feet will swipe on the plastic as if slipping on a shiny oil puddle, and one of us will find ourselves on the ground, maybe bleeding, narrowly avoiding a stray dog's mound of dung a foot from our head. By then everyone will pile water balloons and spray Carioca foam until whoever is on the floor looks like a monster that sheds mounds of shaving cream, the smell of dish soap and faint lavender living on their skin until a shower purges it along with the town's dirt. This introduces the last rule: always cover your face when you become a target. Close your eyes, shut your mouth, use your hands to cup your nose. Because we're fifteen, sixteen, the yearly water fights during Carnival are still fun, and my mother begrudgingly lets me go—as the five of us leave with water balloons and foam cans to roam the streets—and tells us to be careful with the salvajes. The savages. You'd think everyone would be out and about in parades the way Brazilians do, but we don't celebrate with dances, we celebrate with water wars. Most stay at home so they don't get wet. But getting wet is the least of it. They stay home to avoid water balloons' harsh pop of plastic on their bodies. People save up for taxis to prevent getting stained by green ink more radiant than a lizard's viridescent skin. Some get hurt. A friend almost loses an eye one year when a balloon strikes her face as she's sitting in a moving bus, the window open just wide enough to ruin her day. Cyclists get clobbered and collide into jaywalkers, causing a domino effect of gasps and gossip. We know people can be savages, but we're kids and all we want to do is have fun. At first, this is just what happens. A bucket of water from a second floor drenches us, and we dash to a safe corner while saving our balloons for easy targets. Many of the businesses are closed, and the often bike-packed streets have been replaced by taxis that don't honk to see if we need a ride since we're dirty and wet. I hear laughter, *got you!* screams, kids playing with their parents, girls faking anger when dowsed, boys shouting mójala mójala up and down the streets. We stay close, change our trajectory when a large group of men think we can't see their hidden garden hose. After some blocks, we have no more balloons, just enough foam to douse barefoot preteens. We fix each other's runaway hairs, shout when we're about to be bombarded, and wipe the stained mascara from our cheeks. With fingertips soggy, we make our way to a side street where there's just a group of kids playing amongst themselves, too focused on their own battle to pay attention to us. We let our guard down, planning the rest of the path, wondering if we need to head to someone's home to rest and get more foam. I look up toward windows, to the crooks of where walls meet doors, in case someone is waiting to surprise us with a water gun. But I ignore the car speeding on the street while we stroll on the walkway. It's just a driver—no passenger and no windows down. But it's too late once I realize what's happening, and we all shove each other to where our instincts deem is safer, trying to make ourselves small. At first I assume he loses control, but the car halts a foot from us, our hands grabbing another's arms, a chain of linked teenage girls with clothes soaked, skin slimy and damp swarming with goosebumps—not from the water but the fright. He gets out with half the car on the sidewalk, the other half on the street, and glances at us and laughs and laughs and laughs as he strides to a house, moving as quick and slow as watching a water balloon being flung from across the street. My friends shout, call him an animal, a pendejo, while I pull them away in case he races back to do more than a feint. I get a sudden urge to bathe, remove the trail of grime on my neck and the dyes on my skin that I haven't yet seen. Everything feels wrong, as if I know my hair is in disarray, as if I should have stayed dry at home and not sacrificed my least favorite shirt, and I look at my knobby knees and wonder why he wanted to scare us. When we amble to the end of the block—pops of burst pastel plastic littering the pavement—I feel as if we're too grown, maybe not in mind but in bodies, to be playing this game.

Curlicue

When the silver helium balloon ousts the moon,
        another woman is reported missing.
                When omission, don't assume a lie,
        but hold a scorpion in the bathtub
until wilted petals and stem water
        are thrown down the drain
                & a glass vase leads it outside.
When it returns, there is no killing
        but the veil of apparent safety.
                When ingenuous, dusk is an entrance
        for blood dew on dame's rocket.
When upon a cairn, use shears to cut the
        slabs until seeds of sand.
                When the pencil chips, the self-made scars
        on her collarbone fold into origami.
When the peach cavity quivers, a mellisuga
        flutters within the once-sap sphere.
                When the gold eats shadows,
        porcupines long to be touched.
        But only backwards so hands don't bleed.
When bedlam, gates salvage kudzu
        until they become shells for molars.
                When she speaks to a stranger on a street,
        he reaches into his larynx for bolt cutters.

After Frida Kahlo

I don't know what I'd do
if you cut your hair again
and I placed the Autorretrato con Pelo Corto
by my bedside, not knowing that the paint
had made me flesh and I never asked,
but what would you do?
because there is dubious terror in the asking
and silent rage in the response.

In Ecuador,
among rolling hills of arrayán and cuy,
you told me I shouldn't have hair
above my top lip,
not just because I am a woman
but because I'm your esposa,
and I complied the way Kahlo
married Rivera
a year after their divorce,
and when I got back to our home
I called strangers to scorch
lightning on my face
while a puddle of shrieks
pooled into my gums.

I opened our door and through red skin
said look at how much I'll pain
for you because soy tu esposa,
and if we make esposa plural,
it becomes handcuffs,
though I still don't know whose.

And on the day you left,
you could not ask why I had cut my hair
because I'd made sure to keep it rope

long to choke my neck with;
you could not ask why I had hair
on my chin because I'd made sure
to pluck the seeds into our white
rock garden,
so instead you said you needed
to leave because
you don't do your hair anymore

Laceration

When an iguana's tail falls off after a scare,
I've wondered if it feels the pain of a halted human heart
or the shame a woman feels after being sexually assaulted in public.
On many mornings, I've rested on a hammock
below robust mango trees
hoping an iguana didn't fall on me.
If a branch buckled under its weight,
the crack of thin bark would reach me
before I could see a green smear plop onto the ground.

I'd cover my head with my arms
or a book in startled anticipation.
Once, my dog woke from a nap beside me
and began to chase an iguana until it escaped up a tree,
leaving the remnants of its panic behind.
Tiny reptiles left parts of themselves
around my house—shreds of their peeling skin and minute tails—but never green
and black-lined flesh more than a foot long.

It trembled a bit at first, as if it didn't know
yet it had been dislodged from a body,
the cells still hungering for new oxygen.
Eventually, it became still, leaving me
to wonder what threshold of fear
is required for self-amputation.

How many times had I been frightened
enough throughout my life
that a part of me would have severed?

Here I was, with those moments
and my body still with me, although no longer whole,
quivering at times like a loose tail after being chased.

An iguana's stump remains
a wound the first few days
until it slowly begins to mend.
The new tail grows the color
of spoiled lime, darker, like the healing matte of a scab.

The former part of them is out there,
most likely in the spot they were most afraid,
wasting away, and perhaps they look back at this new self,
hoping there'll never be another scare to fragment them once more.
Because—if it were to happen again—
how much of them would be left?

I was on a bus from Guayaquil to Milagro,
and a man sat next to me and began to speak.
I could tell we used to share the same skin color,
but he looked so tan it seemed like he had been chafed
by the sun. He showed me his ID and talked about how he
was a different man from that photo. He had angered his parents
by getting dreads and making the beach his home.
I nodded, looked out the window as if I'd never
seen the fields of banana around us.
Whenever the door opened,
a thick heat engulfed
us as men with
sweat dotting
their lips
sold empanadas withered by the sun.

Before we arrived in my town,
he announced he was getting off.
I was relieved that I could enjoy
some silence for the rest of the ride,
but as he got up, positioned one foot

in the aisle and one in our row,
he grabbed my head with his hands
and collided his mouth with mine.
It happened so fast that I could barely
push him off me, but it was enough
to leave his spit on my lips.
I heard him cackle as he scurried off the bus.

Maybe the difference between an iguana
and me is that although we are both capable of fear,
only one of us is capable of shame. The fear rushed
through me when he was still on me, then came the shame,
and by the time I got to the bus stop, my feelings were tangled in guilt.
I shouldn't have said a word. I should have put on headphones.
I shouldn't have given him a chance.

I wanted to leave my lips behind and grow new ones,
gargle vinegar until my face became numb
and his taste fled my mouth.
Instead, I simmered
myself within
scalding water—
my body
a fragmentation
of what it was
when I woke up
that day.
In the adrenaline
of thoughts, I wished
that my hair
had fallen off
in his hands
as evidence
of what he
took from me.
Take it, I would have said.
May the sever haunt you.

Salt Wounds

I've run ashore for an apology that breezes the windchimes. *Listen to me.* My veins are still saline seeped, and they mistook a bullet for lips. Atonement is a horseshoe crab back tilted. *I apologize. Forget it.* Jade or broken bottles—I can't tell. Walk on your tongue, pace the ligaments. *I'm sorry.* After forgiveness is tawny desert wine—the waitress adds my red-cheeked tear to it. You remind me that I lost your gift: a moss sweater while sunset kayaking. *Just like your father, eh?* This cavity holds castigation. To want an apology is to ask for a snail to make a home in my cochlea. A body or sound, not both. *I already said I'm sorry.* You've dropped your napkin. There's the salt water I choked on when you asked what I want from you. *What else do you want me to say?* To you, sand sucked from my neck. For me, place my head on the seabed and teach me how to gulp without dying.

Synonyms for Betrayal

Crunches of gravel
become my knuckles,
kindle my baby hair
to stop them from
making question
marks on my scalp,
questions he failed
to answer but bore
porcupine quills,
he flattened them
the same way a drip
drip drip becomes
torture 'til succumb
into an abrasion,
'til my meaty lobe
could be seen,
& there I was,
asking the one who
opened the faucet
to make new skin.

Unending

After Jessica Abughattas

all the ways a sentient lie deviates at
when I kneel on the clocks that have been fractured by
the lesson is not that he reeks of
we discover a nutria's skeleton in the wet meadow across
listen to the weeping along
I judge only sitting atop
my withered roses can still be found among
an enduring silence the color of clamor wakes me in the night like
since my dreams have converged between
hold my wisdom to
there seems to be a putrid massacre behind
walk through a fable and into
as I scatter cherry branches of mourning beyond
choose how to curl the toadflax beneath
he holds the pulp juice below
sometimes I sense that the pillow held a coven despite
always wait for the wane to smother the tremble except
above my tongue is what I kept since
let's listen to the acid rain beside
the pale fire leaves a taste through
the silver keeps away the owls from
my mother said to wash my thighs only after

When Prayers Don't Work

If a man stalks by tepid moonlight, we make shadows
weave into arches—fulfill his nightmares
from when he was ten until sleep is a haunting.

In droughts, we sacrifice our palm blood for transient storms.

We pull a nine of swords upside down, leave crystals
under a wolf moon & write with gossamer on mirrors.

We don't use violence, but we let our high voices lead
men to a bear cub dwelling sans honey, mother close.

We break finger bones in the same place they broke
years ago when mended in angles too crooked to be safe.
Leave roadkill on porches that belong to false doctors.

We use gossip as protection when they still roam.

We hide as peregrine falcons behind tipsy women at night
to make sure they get home, body wobbly up the stairs,
head woozy when rum-rest in their beds, only the pain
of a headache following them to tomorrow.

We dig holes to plant teeth, place pomegranates on our spines
& bury locks of hair to make him lose everything.

We burn letters to our former selves with eucalyptus shreds,
compose our future with tips of tincture paper before the smolder.

No roses at funerals, but we offer orchid seeds
for the bereaved, to believe life resides in what can
never be born unless it's hidden in dirt.

Recordation

waived by both parties,
the allegations of the plaintiff's
complaint are proven and correct,
the marriage of the parties has
broken down irretrievably, with no
possibility of reconciliation there are
no children who are issue of
this marriage, the Court further
orders parties' marriage is
dissolved on the grounds of
irretrievable breakdown, the Wife
has instituted an action against the
Husband claiming the dissolution of
marriage and other relief,
binding upon them live separate and
apart from each other, the parties
agree as follows, without
any coercion, now therefore,
hereto as against the other party,
but shall survive the same and be
binding, in the event of the death,
free and clear of any claim by the
Husband, no oral statement or
written matter outside of this
Agreement, an enforceable
contract shall have force or effect,
and so during the terms of their
natural lives

women shouldn't have hair there,
ugh you're too negative, I see how
[redacted], I'm so stupid, why
can't you just say you're lucky to
have me, you're always busy and
can't take just one joke, couldn't
control myself because you
walked into the room, don't take
things so seriously, dress like an
old lady, ways you never said
I truly made you happy, I told you
nothing is wrong, everything is
fine, no I'm not lying, you are
always home & don't like to party
anymore, I should have just
burned the blanket then, is this
what you want, so annoying,
I got you tea two weeks ago, you
never appreciate what I do for
you, everything is fine, he's just a
dog, this house is just a box, I was
only joking, there's nothing to talk
about, I'll watch you from afar,
unfair is what I lived as a kid,
many things in life aren't fair,
that's just how it is, I've been
lying to you, wait 'til
I surprise you, Victoria.

Aftermath

She heard what she wanted to hear,
made cacti into incense sticks
& waited for the smell of palo santo
to seep into her pores,
but there was no fragrance
on the day she asked her therapist:
did you always know I was abused?
& of course the response
was a question in itself:
remember years ago I asked if these events
remind you of your mother and father?
& how will others accept
she has been abused
if she couldn't tell herself
when it was happening,
who would believe her
if she had to write
in her notebook moons later:
log of abusive events—
she blames the ghost fog.
The therapist says
sometimes we accept less abuse
the next time around
because it feels good enough;
a mirage of how you hydrate
through liquor.
I wish he would've hit me.
The response smells of tar:
you wouldn't have left,
the first time is an exception,
a fluke, an anomaly,
not an invitation to leave,
but a hope for redemption,
hail birthed from the ghost fog.
It's not that the sun is gone,

it's that it is hidden.
I thought I was a smart woman.
How could she confuse ammonia
for rain, blood for a diadem,
a weapon for leaf flutters.
How was the beginning?
She wouldn't have stayed
if it began as a ________.
Someone had to explain her life to her.
There are no hematomas,
yes, no pain to show, but it's hidden
in memories of shouts
& what is abuse if it cannot
be post-photographed,
but *this was not your fault,*
sometimes the brain protects
the body from what it already knows
and you weren't ready to see it yet,
she's still making out the view
after downing the fog
with lime & waiting until
the ghouls are no longer blinding.

Part II

Aftermath II

You will listen to coyotes howl underneath willow trees.
You will swim in freezing water with the view
    of the White Mountains stained in a pink silhouette.
You will learn to say no.
You will make fires that last the balmy night.
You will write a poem after a sculpture of a heart
    of sticks and shells born in California.
You will climb a rock face and linger on the vast
    spring landscape from your toes.
You will add tabasco to pulpo gallego and suspend
    yourself on a watermelon drink.
You will save a snapping turtle from traffic on a causeway
    after watching a boat burn from the shore.
You will choose a different color for your lips each day.
You will attend a string quartet when hydrangeas bloom
    azure—& much after—when the wind slits your lips.
You will write ghost stories & some days you'll live them.
You will touch a sloth again.
You will trust what your body tells you: feed me,
    hold me as if I were your house.
You will wonder what the birds are whispering
    to you: great horned owls, red hawks, wild parakeets.
Your hair will soak in cerulean and dry with the help of an eclipse.
You will read this when you remember what came after the enduring.

Still No Rain

My amygdala is with
the tomatoes that are
now rot in the drought
grass, either way the
storms will come,
we'll confuse a sheath
for storm-stripped bark,
nail remnants for anthracite,
erosion for once dog-whelk
tongues—sand will make a
home in the cuticles of my
grey matter, excavate loose
diction, and I've made a
womb on the porch,
waiting for a deer to bow—
to shed its crown of antlers,
not a peace offering,
not a gift, not a knife,
but a reminder we can
let bones grow outside
our bodies too

Eldest Daughter on Her Day Off

She walks to the bronx botanical garden to see the voodoo lily, but more so to make her brain save a new odor that she'd never again like to recall, putrid like burnt books and a past wrong drenched in evermore, because on her day off she decides to use the sense she resorts to less; she's also left her phone at home, and after the whiff, after her neurons create a novel category for this wound scent, she arrives at a café, not a coffee shop—a café—where the menu is in euros and when the waiter arrives she requests anything but the tomato gazpacho her mother forced her to eat when she was ten and vomited in shame—later she learned it was her mother's shame, not hers—and he places a blindfold around her eyes, he says a noun whenever something is ready: *ma'am*, and she finds the glass, brings it to her nose, and it's aniseed, definitely, just not liquor, with a hint of honey and maybe jalapeño flakes, but the last she isn't sure of until some waiting, ah peppercorns, and she downs downs downs, then *sister*, her hands search for the plate, brings her nose close and there's no mistake—peaches—juice dripping on wrists peaches, stain your white shirt specks of fire peaches, and it overpowers so that she can't sense anything else, and decides it's her tongue's turn, and cherry tomatoes twirl, but more so the witchery basil and oh, a surprise, a mound of burrata to balance it out and it's summer in her mouth to her throat, *mothergirl* and it's a gazpacho cucumber, mid-june at six a.m., and she thought she hated gazpacho, but here it is, a lightness of new, of being unencumbered by the past, cool, a decrease in the rhythm of her pulse, *surrogate*: zucchini in garlic sauce and burnt eggplant puree with basil oil—with black garlic ice cream his last word is *matriarch*—blindfold off she has a flashback to when she scuffed her knee on the pavement and she treated it herself, pulled glass with mom's tweezers, knows odor is a catalyst for the past but lets it go, remembers that today is not a date for flashbacks but for this, this now, she tips and teletransports to the beach and for once she shows her midriff, waits until the sea stays on her scalp, salt is like an eldest daughter she thinks, it can keep others from spoiling, adds taste, lends itself to liquor, it can disappear metal just like she can, why are you so salty, because on her day off she smells flora, eats swollen fruits, and licks salt at the beach, and when she goes home, she has more missed calls than iris layers, and she decides that it can all wait 'til tomorrow

Body Nest

On my tongue

live waxwings,

frenulum as

twisted root,

papillae as

sustenance,

mother visits

with trill songs

& in swallow a

hatchling sifts

down my throat,

trachea pulls the

chick to mouth

light—a remnant

feather cascades

to wrap the crevices

of this trunk stem.

Has Anyone Asked the Momma Bear Whether She Prefers Man or Bear?

In the woods one day, I stumble upon a bear,
    & she asks that I walk with her to find her lost
        cubs, & we look for missing marigolds,
            clawed trees, & the sweet smell of baby bear breath,
& when I come upon a bush of rosary peas,
    she points out their black bloodshot would convince
        me that I have eyes on my palms before my bowels slay me.
            She tells me elder tales of being wary,
fear of raw hide & bullets to make her fur into a souvenir,
    & she says we'll stop if she smells wet dog,
        not because of the dog, but that means a man is near.
            How do you do it? She asks. *What?*
Live with men.
    Me? Well, I pretend, I say, as I scramble to a lookout,
        Pretend that they'll change. That if he's unsure
            a berry is poison, he won't feed it to me.
Pretend quiet is tenderness & not punitive silence.
    Pretend predator & protector overlap.
        Then we hear a whimper. In a slim cave are Hopper
            & Jules, & when mom licks them out,
they say there were voices. Haggard, grimy,
    enflamed accents. We nod. We look up, see the sun blaring
        & an opposite slither of the moon doused in its heat.
            They lead me back to the trail, the babies lick
my temple & then they let me be.

Stay in Your Throat

The man's remark was like many others,
though we'd heard his voice before—in his
house—as we gossiped with his daughter. But now
our thighs were thicker, eyes silver-shadowed. I wanted
recognition to shine in his irises. An apology to escape his lips.
For the softness of a girl's skin to stay in his throat. But the only thing
in his stare was the hollow of us as unfamiliar, and a veneer of eager—
waiting
        for us to
                be replaced by
                        other legs,
                                a new sight.

Aftermath III

After she is murdered
and before her mother
can identify her body,
a foreman takes a photo
and shares

shares shares shares shares
shares shares shares shares shares shares
shares shares shares shares shares shares shares
shares shares shares shares shares shares
shares shares shares shares shares shares shares
shares shares shares shares shares shares shares
shares shares shares shares shares shares
shares shares shares shares shares shares shares
shares shares shares shares shares shares shares shares shares shares shares
shares shares shares shares shares her body

after a town lawyer
says it was an *error*
in judgment and, after,
the same repentant
plea is uttered: he is a
father who has

a daughter a daughter a daughter a daughter a daughter
a daughter a daughter a daughter a daughter a daughter
a daughter a daughter a daughter a daughter a daughter
a daughter a daughter a daughter a daughter a daughter a
daughter a daughter a daughter a daughter a daughter a daughter a daughter a daughter a
daughter
a daughter a daughter a daughter a daughter a daughter a daughter
a daughter a daughter a daughter a daughter a daughter
a daughter a daughter a daughter a daughter a daughter
a daughter

after the common statement
that men cannot injure,
maim, hurt, ruin—
if they have sisters
and wives
and daughters
because proximity
somehow equates
benevolence
instead of a
demonstration of

possession possession possession possession possession
possession possession possession possession possession possession
possession possession possession possession possession possession
possession possession possession possession possession possession
possession possession possession possession possession
possession possession possession possession possession
possession possession possession possession possession possession
possession possession possession possession possession possession possession
possession possession possession
possession possession possession possession

before him was a
bound woman who
had lost her life,
take even more
from her in death,
as if he owned
an object, a thing,
a shell, and after
the town decides
not to press charges

press charges press charges press charges press charges press charges press charges press
charges press charges press charges press charges press charges
press charges press charges press charges press charges press charges
press charges press charges press charges press charges press charges press charges
press charges press charges press charges press charges
press charges press charges press charges press charges press charges press
charges press charges press charges press charges press charges
press charges press charges press charges press charges
press charges press charges
press charges

and after years
of driving by Greenwich,
where she was found,
to New Rochelle,
where she is from,
I still say a prayer
for Valerie

and put a curse
curse
curse
curse
curse
curse
curse
curse
curse
curse
curse
curse
curse on you all.

Iterations of Self(Portrait)

Sometimes I meditate or my mind
wanders
to a coincidental elevator meeting
with all the men who have tasted me.
I listen to hard-core classical music
on the way to the island
where I first heard my voice out loud.
I do not know how to spell necesary
without checking the dictionary.
My revenge includes the unborn
& seaside beach towns.
These tears have never made a river
but they have drenched
into a swollen pond.
I learned the word *covet*
watching Silence of the Lambs.
I'm convinced
my dreams
are
messages.
My lip is pretty
because a cat slashed it
when I had more bones.
I'm worried I mistake memories
for ideational nuance.
My former husband
used to shame
me for crying.
Yes, I've eaten a bunny.
I had my first period
when I was nine.
Learning to love myself
began the same age
that Jesus was when he was killed.
Did he love himself? I ask sometimes.

I don't have a favorite word in English.
I keep dresses
I don't fit into anymore
as a burial
to my former shape.
I used to smoke
to punish myself,
but I did not know this
until much later.
Sex stopped hurting when I was 34.
I'm convinced my dreams
are tying loose ends
of an ingrained mystery.
I'm afraid to take a test
online to see whether I have ADHD.
I ceased trying to control my tears.
Most days, I look at myself
in the mirror and say: "I love you."
Some days I mean it.

I did not have a favorite word in English

but I have chosen the word fuck due to its versatility. It is very much a fucking choice. In Spanish, it's libélula, make sure you pronounce it with the emphasis on the be. Like, sometimes I choose to be fucked; not get fucked. Like on the day my dog died I chose not to call my ex. If my father taught me anything was to be sweet and petty. Think me a sick fuck? Nope, I'm at peace. To be called a fucking bitch is not a surprise to me. I did call my therapist after I cradled his lifeless body and even she agreed: fuck him. Though she didn't say that, more so: *I agree with you that's not a good idea.* My mom? She said: *Why would you fucking call him?* Look at how many fucks I give. I used to. I used to give all the fucks. I used to fuck with him—an international flight, a bus, a taxi, an Uber, and we pulled the fuck up to his long-lost father's office. After meeting his son for the first time, the man said *I need to go see 'bout some chickens.* Insert all forms of expletives here, in noun and adjective form. Just like the word fuuuuuck can be adoptable in all situations, and even in adverb form, it was thoroughly employed on that day and thereafter. But, fuck, that's before I knew the apple doesn't fall too far from the chicken farm. It's funny how the most vulgar people would wince at an uttered fuck. The Comstock Act passed in 1873 made it unlawful to print the word fuck. But saying it feels so good and printing it makes it less elusive, more permanent, heartier. If my dad taught me anything is that there's a time and place for everything, even using the term fuckwad needs to be employed with the right audience and at the most opportune instance. For example, did you know that the work fuck is said more than 230 times in the film *The Departed?* I love that fucking film. *What's the matter, smartass, you don't know any fuckin' Shakespeare?* Every good film is about betrayal. Every good fucked-up story that stays with you has a rat. That should have prepared me, but you don't know what the fuck you don't know, right? You might think I play too fucking much. Absofuckinlutely.

Does the Devil Send Gifts?

She asks me over the phone—and I think of Pandora's box, how it's always the woman's curiosity that wreaks havoc—not the maker of the box, but the one who releases it; for me, the fault lands on Zeus, always Zeus—and there's that time there were flies lingering on my plate the day of my grandfather's funeral, nothing but devil sent, I thought—and of course I never went back to that restaurant again—but have you seen the devil, at least in *Bedazzled*, God is a Black man and the devil a white woman in stilettos, and I've never seen better representation than that, because they're sitting down for a game of chess laughing while moving pawns and sipping espressos, and both are wearing white, because in that scene red would be too much of a cliché and I'm sure if we saw them we wouldn't recognize them, and a gift that was definitely devil sent was a tape recorder I recorded myself saying bad words to when I was twelve and then couldn't delete so off to the garbage it went, and yes, I still feel guilty two decades later, and I really want to ask this lady what type of gift she means, maybe a colibrí outside her window telling her she needs to pour salt over shoulder for protection—a colibrí means hummingbird but in my other language the word sounds so much better—and is that something the devil would say, I wonder, and I want to ask her even more, like do you think you'll know if it's a gift from the devil because he's been around a lot longer than we have and how could you possibly tell, and I envision a gift on my porch wrapped in blue velvet and a tag that says *to Victoria from the Devil* in 18th century penmanship, and I'd probably open it thinking it's an ex-boyfriend trying to play a trick on me to find that inside there is nothing but air—that the box is the gift itself—and I realize I am still on the line, and if I say anything I want to say this might be a one-hour conversation or if I say the wrong thing, I'll get reported, and well, they don't pay me enough to answer questions about the devil so I take a breath and say all that's expected of me: *I don't know, but I'll pray for you.*

i pledge allegiance

to venus dimples & under-arm
whitening cream & tweezers
& mirrors that will not be used
to see if my mole is, perchance,
now cancer but if my back has rolls,
vampire facials to avoid lines
that say i've touched grass
for too long & there should be no
hair on knobs or in nose,
& the skin above my lips
should only be home to skin,
an hourglass can tell time
& this body must not,
paint fingernails the color
of his lust, not the satin silver
that makes you wish,
& there should be no mounds,
but breasts, tender, no aureola
whiskers—& most of all I pledge
allegiance to pain so he can love
the parts of me I never knew
I had to change

Ode to Ruby

I have named the osprey
that lives by the I-95
on a lined castle of a
transmission tower,
regal puff chest, nest
tighter than jaws,
seen almost daily on
my way to & from work:
          Ruby,
not because you belong
to me, but because somehow
in the perils of this grief
I have come to belong to you.
To gaze upon me; O, what
accidents have you seen?
          Ruby,
I know you love a good
brawl, could have picked
anywhere to lay babes
but at a highway bend
is where you so chose.
How loud is it when there's
no traffic, when halts ease,
when I do not drive by to
surrender my day to you?
          Ruby,
why nest in the middle
of ruckus? Is it you want
to show off your wingspan,
to remind us that we are
confined to the commute
& your man, who shall remain
nameless, feeds you trout?
At first I can't tell you apart

in flight, but alas, you're
thicker, mightier—
O, I miss you when you're
gone, a surge of fear
in absence, golden mornings,
but I catch you in midsoar
tomorrow, as if saying,
honey, worry for what?
          Ruby,
Are you scared of thunder?
I'm not, but I think of you
when bolts & lights & storms,
I've seen you, summer down
pour, on eggs, but somehow
I know you are not drenched,
that you were born for this.
Come August, when the sweet
sadness of mellowed heat
comes, I prepare myself.
Your departure—inevitable—
as constant as your posture.
          Ruby,
men have beeped at me,
they want to get on, so do I,
but I always slow to catch a
glimpse, to hold my head in
reverence, it's been a few
years now, my life looks
different from the first
moment I gazed upon you,
O, I wait for you, your nest
is always there, a reminder
in leafless and whiteouts:
we always come home.

Mami Says

men only want one thing. They will take it and huir,
    as if my body were a flesh fantasma
        they keep tabs on in their pocket.
I don't say that one time is enough sometimes.
    That each one kisses the corner of my neck
        with a different head tilt. That I do not want
más after our skin shares sweat.
    I don't say it's a different time, another century.
        I say *Bueno, Mami*, and save the words for a future
daughter: primero, sex is pleasure. To touch
    and to part can be exactly what two people need.

An Etymology II

Heartbreak should be called bodybreak,
look, I learned how to break my body
before I knew words for it, before I
learned the etymology of *break*
is connected to *brick* and *brake*,
before I knew that in English it
meant *of bones*, before I read the words
destroy continuity, listen, a shaman
once connected to my body & asked
me how I withstood the pain,
by breaking, but I didn't know that yet,
& all I said is yes, someone believes
this broken pain, appetite of what,
my stomach lining ate itself,
maybe accepted a strawberry
but nothing that would peak,
like anticuchos, figs, or starch,
I ate ice, the feel of it hard,
the lump of it almost food,
when liquid ices it spreads
out like an enchantress' arthritis,
hear me out, I became hungry
again when the shaman said I'd
be alive in ten years, learned to
make food into currency,
until it tasted like gold, until I
stopped wanting to become a
cessation, until the fulness
asked me to only break bread

Lists I Make in Process of Divorce

budget money
budget the number of teeth that break in my dreams
self-help books I read
arson fantasies
the plants he left
how many ravens have conversations on my daily walks
days I eat
the new plants I decorate with
amount of times I hear the word toxic
monthly budget
lawyer fees
times I see the osprey I've named Ruby off the I-95
possible lies and definite lies
amount of times coyotes wake me while camping at the Buddhist temple
cost of therapy
quartet concerts
times he screams in my dreams
days I don't take Ambien
the ways financial sacrifices require stillness
paid sick days
times my mom cries with me
face licks by my dog to trap my tears
days I find myself on the floor crying
ways to love myself
fighting words
free forms of self-care
days of no contact
nights I sleep more than three hours
times I remind myself that grief isn't linear
days in a row I meditate
pictures of us I find when I thought no more existed
days since I last wrote
days lost
days learning

days unlearning

days I wake up in the remembrance of nightmares

the times I live each day without lurking into days past

Questions for My Grief

you leave in the shape of a moth and come back as sandstone tongs to scrape the cancellous from my pelvis / oh here, would you also like an abalone scalpel with that / i cannot keep up with the shape sound of you / the tethered flags tearing onto themselves on my morning walks / can't you see that i'm tired of the way it snows in june / do you like being here and napping within my uvula / waking up in the void where he used to sleep with his back turned to me / i see you leaving again, the breadcrumbs he left still in my mane / wait, can you let me know when you'll be back / if i'll fail to recognize you at first / then feel you scuff the dry skin from my lips to feed it to me / i'll never be ready, but i'd like to be prepared / please /

Brain Confit

I want to know what brains taste like. The trite of memories left under the sun for too long. Cherries turned into carnation pus. The hard of liver blood in soft muscle. If the hippocampus is cut, how will the sulci taste without the attachment to memories? Perhaps the harshness of a bit lip tumbling onto perennial ryegrass. Seeped in caramelized onions or deep fried with shallots as decoration. And if made from a stranger's hand or, rather, someone I love? A quiver of sour from the first. Maybe the parietal lobe resembles the gamy of lamb if concocted from a spouse's hand—or a lick of silt with a layering of storm rain. My buds may expand in aversion to let my insular cortex know: please, never again. A novel taste sprouting within old memories of a chicken heart I once spit out to let a zaguate indulge in. I've had fermented chicha, blood sausage caldos made tender with lime, the tough lining of the stomach in a syrupy garlic-peanut sauce, a salty filling of tripita mishqui, ceviche de concha where the soup resembled a puddle but the taste stimulated all my senses in desire. I've devoured plenty, but there's still so much my mouth wants. I don't know what brains taste like, but my tongue lies patient, waiting to be fed sautéed twists of bound hemispheres.

French Nails in Dirty Red ft. Gold Chrome

On the day my husband leaves
he says he's leaving because
I don't do my nails, hours after
he said he loved me, minutes after
he said he was lying last night
& also the last three years,
in the next months I look at
my nails, naked, my therapist
says he didn't leave because
of that, still I look at them,
their simplicity, at my ring finger,
where the indent of my wedding
& engagement rings take months
to disappear, I swing between
extremes, letting them chip because
they do not determine who I am,
or painting them every week, silver,
hot pink, blackened purple, & I
stare at them, sometimes giggle,
thinking this *this* is what was
important, the façade of it all,
within a year a friend learns
gel nail art & for my birthday
she creates a unique design
for me, a distinct flower on every
nail, a lily on my left index,
tulip on a pinky, lavender
on a thumb, I tell her I seldom
get my nails done, they rarely
last a week, & she says *don't use*
your nails as tools, so simple,
& the next days I catch myself
trying to use my nails to scratch
my hairline, pressing buttons
on a remote, tapping as a refuge

from boredom, fine tools to open
a can of cherries, & I stop, my tasks
take longer than before, let the plump
of my fingers do the work,
an excuse to slow, to decide now they
are decoration, my friend helps me
tell a story with my nails, & I ask
for a french manicure in black,
but on that day she says it's the
summer & I'm going to the beach,
why not dirty red? & on the edge
of the red is a golden chrome
that ovals to my cuticles,
& everywhere I go, dentists,
maybe wives, gynecologists,
maybe divorcées like me, ask
to see my nails, cup my hands
in theirs, ask me questions,
& I delight in their curiosity,
my favorite design is a request
for evil eye nails, pinkies
holding the blued eyes, index
with a bright star, the ring
fingers have a loose french tip
made of a confluence of blue,
a slush of a wave after its crescendo
separated from the rest of the nail
with a wiggle of gold chrome,
the index with a tiny evil eye &
sparking gold paper, sometimes
I look down, forget these are my
hands, that my nails have become
cat-eye long, & the weekend
the evil eyes are set, I go camping,
set up the tent in the slowest time,
buy bundles of wood & haul them
to the campsite, cook with portable
fuel & hold my books under

a flashlight, & by the end of the trip
there's no chip, no break, because
my nails aren't tools, I've learned,
not a tool to make my ex-husband
happy or to pull ice from a tray,
oh yes, my ex-husband, you may
have forgotten him by now, I sure
did. I know nothing about him—
my nails sure look pretty, though.

a sestina on an early childhood education

play a lasting lullaby on an organ for your rage,
a girl dances! a girl wants! a girl's desire!
wait to become a woman in blood flood,
or before that, when a street walk is combat,
you must learn all before you wake;
still, did you weep when curtsied into a bow?

decorate crumbs & after i'll teach you to bow
to the spire that holds light-candied rage,
dress ken in a hawaiian shirt during barbie's wake,
remember! as a woman! never inquire about desire!
learn that your voice can crawl him to combat,
ha! power? you plead to command a molasses flood.

a brush fire doesn't always wash away a flood
& your head can't hold a crown, only a lethal bow,
a woman! can be too toy! with friendly combat!
in the anatomy of your teeth, the pulp caresses rage,
don't touch yourself—a body is not a temple for desire,
use your tongue to push a boulder to your master's wake.

be as sure as a rampant river that you want to wake,
because in your mouth there's always a flood,
do not long, do not want to endure in desire,
you can bow to him but what matters are your hair bows
and lip liner! and you can only scream! at a rave rage!
because no one likes to hear a voice mired in combat.

underestimate your taste! & what you can combat!
make sure you listen when he orders you to wake
the girls that don't know the definition for rage,
but who know that crying shimmer is the only flood
they can create with their bodies—an arrow, a bow,
a sword, with all of these you'll try to replace desire.

tell me, what will you beg for, if not desire?
or maybe the right to use astilbe in combat,
do not confront the way his head refuses to bow,
it's safer to be a girl in a dream than to wake
as a woman, & the opposite of a flood
is not a drought but the talent to withhold rage.

no, you can't choose vinyl dreams, time to wake
up, be good & find mom's lost stilettos in the after flood,
i promise you that growing up is all! the! rage!

Therapy Speak

Throw a stone at a boundary and the receiver will either cut a cot on it or leave with it in her pocket until its weight is ignored for common baggage. Soft belly breaths to reach a periphery and with the strands of carbon are the shavings he asked her to cook pinto with. The difference between fantasy and reality is a repressed memory of a pigeon pretending to be a swan. The whiteness secluding the nothing of *I can't remember, it didn't happen*, but her esophagus knows it did. Trigger her into an octopus using shells as temporary armor and all that she wants is ironic and subtle. In the unconscious, the bumblebees assassinate the queen. Somatic feeling is nothing when she eats her fingerprints past the ridges. Holds her breath by tadpoles and waits until they feed on distress tolerance. Gaslight, oil light, only sees the light when she is no longer seeped in it. To write with only pages as an audience, only the cortex as a hat tipper. Sometimes her anger wakes in the crust of her left knee, but danger always lives in the sweet of her intestines. And she learns to differentiate between crisis and distress and danger but her primitive brain—still in a cave, still gathering mushrooms—for it it all feels the same, but she remembers this is just the intellectuality of it all, and she forgets to feel sometimes, until she stops her sitz bones and gives each emotion a shape, and sometimes naming is the first moment she knows it'll all be a l r I g h t.

When I Die, Do Not Mention My Labor

But how I read by knives during apagones,
United *lynx* and *zephyr* in Scrabble,
Searched for cyan and Milky Way with suckle,
Made hexes & karma connive as cousins,
Saved my curls as I vomited celadon,
Three-night stand with Brian & at a decade's pass, still wink emojis.
How I tanged jocotes with fermento mori;
O, how I've eaten and woven hips.
Remember my eyes tasted of spice,
Vivaldi's seasons made my spine into a verb,
That scar curve on my lips a wound beauty mark,
Jacarandas bowed to me on crux walks,
I confused dreams with echoes, & love for açai,
No labor
          —but I did sway in slingbacks off a cliff.

Woman Takes Revenge

My favorite quote from high school
is mi pluma lo mató from an Ecuadorian
politician about another politician, and I
swipe right on profiles that say *not political*
because I can't speak with someone based
on a negation of reality, because yes,
everything is political is a cliché because it's true,
because going to the courthouse
and sharing an elevator with a former abuser
is political because so is that it takes a woman
an average of seven times to leave intimate
partner violence and in the hours and days
after she leaves is when she is most capable
of being murdered, because so is Gisèle's choice
to have a public trial, *Wife takes public revenge*
says the headline—if a trial is revenge, what is justice?
So is that the judge reminds her not to use the word *rape* but *sex scene*,
to protect the presumption of innocence, while recordings of the rapes were found
in a folder labeled *abuse*, and it is merely September,
Gisèle will walk into court, sit in front of her (alleged) rapists—until December,
and 'til now French politicians have been mum,
an exception is Sandrine Josso, a politician who says another politician
drugged her last year to rape her, allegedly, remember, allegedly—
and more than eighty men, forty-nine on trial, one charged
in absentia, and not one called the police, not one called
her,
even an anonymous phone call could have saved my life,
all men, even the ones who refused to rape,
remained silent,
Gisèle, my hero, no pen with which to slay—
but may your voice annihilate them.

Poem for my Revenge Poems

I water them with lemon ginger tea and sweat;
they carry clubs and my deep undoings, becomings,
sometimes a whisper sounds like a plight of loose ends.
Perhaps they've committed wrongs mired in righteous rites,
ask questions when I created them to answer,
may seem heavy but somersault as feathers,
always untangle my incisors 'til glisten
with the same comb they use to ripen scar tissue.
While I sleep, they cross the bridge, light my past wildfire,
eat bizcochos with rum and unseek forgiveness
from anyone but themselves, no God but guffaws,
bring me a sparrow skull—a treat of nectar neb,
taught me poems can't kill, but they sure can wound—
their mother's name is Victoria for a reason.

Eight Months Post Divorce

The tree bark
beckons me for a hug,
and I hang on
until I feel a pulse.
With soiled boots
upon the spring
a common brimstone
flutters a praise
of *you're here,*
you came here,
walk with me;
there is no possession
to hold its float near,
linger 'til its vanishing
along the light tincture.
In the burr of the trail,
wild chives beg to be seen.

On my knees again,
barring angst pleads,
I refuge the roots
with my fingers,
gold ring dank,
far away dripfall,
and it rises
from the vena cava,
damp into chest fill,
ascent beyond the neck,
it sweeps into a quiver,
no need to combat it
into suppression,
despair weeps
and delight tears
sound the same sob
to the silver maples,
but here, stirring the earth,
I know the difference.

Origin

Ravens rest by our necks,
claws dot blood on our shoulders,
caw us to madness and half sleep—
my neighbors drink stale coffee
by crimson king maples as their ravens

cock fight before work and in aftermath:
both men wave, blood on a lapel, a dead raven
on the ground, another in triumphant loop flight,
my faint wave from the kitchen window,
and how to free ourselves when we're always

being watched, even in dreams their cloak eyes
bubble, eat the wax from our ears until we
scream awake—even when I bathe my children,
it bounces from shoulder to my shoulder,
leaves cola caps by the lice shampoo,

no tears not as in cry, no tears as in no hair rips,
and if you murder one then another takes its place,
on frigid mornings storms fuss in rain feathers
without the thunder, and Nelia asks me if she was born
in an egg, did she poke herself out or eat herself inside

to outside shell, where is her baby raven, but I say hush,
you are still allowed just your body, wing flaps
by your cheeks a mystery, flesh un-refuged,
you'll get one in due time, and others have wanted
to pretend at being masters, named a raven Polly

and fed it berries dipped in yogurt, tried to make it
speak but all that they emit are ghoul hums
with bark scratch for a voice, and beaks so close
to the neck that they are our gods, when one day
my husband and Nelia and Adrian are gone,

while slicing red bell peppers and tomato
and rosemary that need to be ready for my
family's arrival, I take it from its beak
and sever the neck just right, let it bleed,
pluck the feathers, and alas dinner,

and by the time they come home,
all sitting by the table, a winged gathering
has surrounded our house, and glass pecks
are worse than tree bark pecks,
and my son Adrian says my back is straight,

my chin pecks are healing, and Nelia asks
why they want to get in, where is my mother raven,
and I say eat, my children, this will be the last full meal
in a while, because mommy will be too tired to get up from bed,
I say tired because they don't know the meaning of wounded,

and my husband pretends there is no sound, and we wait for them
to break in, and maybe they'll get drunk off my blood wine,
and when they cannot lunge in flight, we can all grow wings
in the form of knives and devour all this murder with a hint
of brandy so my children's jugulars can remain free

Rhetorical Analysis: A 21st Century Courting Sample*

Not to be cocky, but I'm really the full package—my love language is gentle bullying—don't care about your career or how strong or independent you can be, can you be a wife? Hummus over sex. Looking for someone that elicits sufficient oxytocin levels to activate reward centers in my prefrontal cortex. Sarcasm. This world of fake ass, plastic hair, and pretty face filters. I'm not a sexual deviant. Dark humor. If you're crazy, stay away. I will beat up your ex for you. Please, no pronouns. If we can't roast each other, I don't want it. Don't play with me, play with your kitty. Sarcastic. If I use a superlike on you, and you don't swipe right, kindly Venmo me $2.99. Looking for a woman with a good sense of humor. I'm like Drake in every way. Let's build an empire. Normal guy, just not going to write an essay. This is exhausting. Drama free, low-maintenance guy. I thought bitches love dogs. Not here to waste time. Must be able to take sarcasm, kicked off Tinder over a joke. I don't even care if you're a murderer or have an Android at this point. Let's wrestle. What's your resume? I'm just trying to have a real family and my ex ruined that so. Looking for someone who can control a room. Ted Bundy in the sheets. Please don't waste my time. Just make sure you feed me. I hate people. I'm not here for you; I'm here for me, until you become important enough for me.

**This is a found poem written with the biographical content from men on Bumble and Hinge profiles within a twenty-five-mile radius of my location.*

To Heal in Guanacaste

This mends with sea swells and lush-salted skin,
deep by the estuary to soothe these bones.

Soothing waves spill secrets estuary deep
to savor ayote in tamarindo sauce.

Be your own savior on Tamarindo sand,
letting bygones rest with the howler monkeys.

Rest now, let the smirked sloth haul what ails,
there is much hibiscus to feed soul and lips.

Sol sweetened hibiscus to nurse colibris,
the waves take what they want & leave me whole.

The whole of me leaves with the wave curls;
notice the scent silence by the lemon trees.

Tree scent, lemon aid & no more silencing;
this mends with sea swells and lush-salted skin.

Waxing Gibbous

I used an axe to count these pumice ribs,
sabotaged my spine into lily pads,
before I knew that you *play* piano
in English—not *touch*—like in my first tongue.
Since then I've learned to suck bone marrow,
leave my hair to dry on a clothesline
in a crown of lavender & a wasp den,
wash my skin in lilac milk and whisper
sweets—thick as alfajores that ripple
to the permanent paths of my whisked palm;
my navel holds the honey, crisp light lines
on my ass have names: *Gretel*, *Amira*,
basking in the sun, the moon wants a peek,
the first time I love me when no one sees.

Acknowledgments

The author is grateful to the editors of the following literary magazines in which work has appeared, at times in different iterations:

A Review of My Birth Control Methods in *The Normal School*

Body Nest in *The Lickety Split*

Corpse Dress in *Stanchion Zine*

Daddy's Lesson in *Mythic Picnic*

Does the Devil Send Gifts? in *The Westchester Review*

Fragile in *Versification Zine*

Game Over in *Ellipsis Zine*

How to Sleep Alone as a Woman in *Cottonxenomorph*

Inherited Rituals in *Autofocus Literary*

Laceration in *X-R-A-Y Literary Magazine*

Mainstream Outlets in *Alebrijes Review*

Mami Says in *The Offing*

Natasha Romanoff Died Because She Had No Kids or Spouse in *The Daily Drunk Magazine*

Nature's Classroom in *Lumiere Review*

Stay in Your Throat in *Ran Off With the Star Bassoon*

Still No Rain received an honorable mention for *Connecticut River Review*'s 2023 Vivian Shipley Contest

After Frida Kahlo is written in response to the painting *Autorretrato con pelo corto (Self-portrait with cropped hair)* by Frida Kahlo-1940. Oil on canvas 40 x 28 cm. Museum of Modern Art of New York City, New York, USA.

Borsuk, Ken. "Greenwich DPW Worker Took Photos of Murder Victim." *Greenwich Time*, 7 Feb. 2019, www.greenwichtime.com/local/article/Greenwich-investigates-whether-DPW-worker-took-13598822.php.

Conradi, Peter. "France's Rape Case: The Week That Put a Nation on Trial." *Thetimes.com*, The Sunday Times, 7 Sept. 2024, www.thetimes.com/article/france-rape-case-trial-dominique-pelicot-wife-7z5nxzdt6.

Even Beyoncé Said She Raised Her Man is written in response to the song: Beyoncé, "JOLENE," *Cowboy Carter*, Parkwood Entertainment and Columbia Records, 2024.

Hartford Courant. "Greenwich Municipal Worker Who Photographed Body of Homicide Victim Valerie Reyes Demoted by Town." *Hartford Courant*, Hartford Courant, 21 Mar. 2019, www.courant.com/2019/03/21/greenwich-municipal-worker-who-photographed-body-of-homicide-victim-valerie-reyes-demoted-by-town/.

How to Sleep Alone as a Woman is a found poem written with responses to a question I posed on X (formerly Twitter) about how others prepare to sleep alone as a woman.

Inherited Rituals is a collaborative piece written with Grecia Huesca Dominguez.

Not Saturn Devouring His Son is in response to the painting *Saturn Devouring His Son* by Francisco Goya. 1820–23. Museo del Prado, Madrid, Spain.

Rhetorical Analysis: 21st Century Courting Sample is a found poem written with the biographical content from men on Bumble and Hinge profiles within a twenty-five-mile radius of my location. It is inspired by the Burned Haystack Method, which was created by Jennie Young.

The epigraph is from Mónica Ojeda. "Historia de la leche." *Temporales*. New York University, December 2020. https://wp.nyu.edu/gsas-revistatemporales/historia-de-la-leche-poemas-de-monica-ojeda/.

To Heal in Guanacaste is written in the form of a duplex, a poetic form invented by Jericho Brown.

Unending is written in response to the poem "Litany for My Father" by Jessica Abughattas.

Thank you to my Higher Power.

Eternal gratitude to Octavio Quintanilla and TRP.

I'm grateful to the Connecticut Office of the Arts, Craigardan, GrubStreet, Sundress Academy for the Arts, Tin House, Kitchen Table Literary Arts, and VONA for encouraging my work in a myriad of ways. This book would have been an impossibility without their support.

A heartfelt thanks to Carol Ann Davis, Frederick-Douglass Knowles II, and Ana Maria Spagna for their kind words in support of this book.

Many of these poems arose or were edited in workshops led by Elizabeth Acevedo, Diannely Antigua, Dorothy Chan, Chen Chen, Joan Kwon Glass, Octavio Quintanilla, and Roy G. Guzmán. Much gratitude to each of you and your guidance.

Thank you to Reinaldo Kevin Buitron, Jr., Madeline DeLuca, Emily Dillon, Chelsea Dodds, Joey Gould, Grecia Huesca Dominguez, Marcela Maldonado, Angelike Páez, and Juan Carlos Porras for being the first to read my poems in their early stages. I appreciate you and our unique friendships so much.

For those who uplifted me during this process: María Alejandra Barrios, María Fernanda Freire, Sonya Huber, Kenisha Jones, Janay Jordan, Julia López, Faith Marek, Millie McMaster, Charlene Nigro, Juliette Páez, Adriana Páramo, Valeria Pólit, Katie Schneider, and Karen Vasquez. Thank you, thank you, thank you.

Immense gratitude to my dear friends who have opened the doors to their homes so that I could have a quiet place to write and edit this book: Betsy and Kevin Buckley, Christopher Madden and Carol Sutton, Phil and Sarah DiGennaro, Alba Riofrío, Juan Carlos Porras and Estuardo del Valle, Marcela Maldonado and Ben Mertz, and Meghan Muldowney.

To Angie, my best friend, for being there with me since '08.

Thank you to my mother and father for reminding me to believe. In myself. In my strength. In my words.

And an abundance of gratitude to you, reader. This book made its way to you because it's for you.

About the Author

VICTORIA BUITRON is a writer who hails from Ecuador and resides in Connecticut. She received an MFA in Creative Writing from Fairfield University. She is currently the Competitions Editor for *Harbor Review*. Her work has appeared or is forthcoming in *Southwest Review*, *Stanchion Zine*, *Shenandoah*, *Cutleaf*, and *HuffPost*, among others. Her debut memoir-in-essays, *A Body Across Two Hemispheres*, was the 2021 Fairfield Book Prize winner. Her flash fiction was selected for 2022's *Best Small Fictions* and *Wigleaf's Top 50*. In 2023, she received the *Artistic Excellence Award* from the Connecticut Office of the Arts, which also receives funding from the National Endowment for the Arts, a federal agency. She is currently working on a novel about love, violence, and betrayal.

VersoFrontera

Series Editor: Octavio Quintanilla

In collaboration with the VersoFrontera Literature and Arts Festival, the VersoFrontera series seeks to publish one debut full-length collection per year by an emerging poet.

BOOKS IN THIS SERIES:

No. 001—Victoria Buitron—*Unburying the Bones*